Average to Awesome

Average to Awesome:

Transitioning from Where You Are to Where You Want to Be

Tim Bowers

ISBN-13: 978-1539899389

Cover design: Gabrielle Montgomery

DEDICATION

This book is dedicated to:

Lucille Bowers (mom), thank you for not giving up when times got tough. Thank you for being a super woman who raised six boys and two girls. Thank you for being an example of how to persevere when all odds are against you. Thank you for your love and being a praying mother.

Nieces and nephews:

You were not born to be average. You were born to leave a legacy worth remembering.

Brothers and Sisters:

Mark Bowers, Kenny Bowers, Calvin Bowers, John Bowers, Rayshell Bowers, Teresa Bowers and James Bowers. I love y'all!

Allendale Community: This is for the youth, students and young adults who think what they want out of life is impossible.

My mentor Jabari Dunbar: You are not here to celebrate all my achievements but I thank you for your guidance and mentorship. Thank you for helping me see it doesn't matter where I come from, I can still succeed. You inspired me to be great.

Contents

ACKNOWLEDGMENTS

This book would have not come into fruition without some people directly or indirectly inspiring, motivating and coaching me along the way. I would like to give a special thank you to Tamika Sims for walking me through the process of writing my first book.

Dr. Leslie Bessellieu for challenging me to think outside the box and giving me so many resources that contributed to my personal development.

Kendall Ficklin for helping me stay motivated to navigate through difficult times.

The Benedict College Service-Learning and Leadership Development "White House" family for their encouragement, love and support in any endeavor I pursued.

Darrin Thomas for introducing me to what hard work looks like. I'm not sure if there's a person on this planet that can out-work him.

Michelle Grimes and Johnny Grimes of the Word of God Church and Ministries for your love and support and always being available when I needed spiritual guidance.

To everyone who listened to a chapter, offered suggestions or constructive criticism, I can't thank you enough!

FOREWORD

Having read many life changing books early in my career such as *"The Magic of Thinking Big"* – Dr. David J. Schwartz and *"Think and Grow Rich – A Black Choice"* - Dr. Dennis Kimbro (and Napoleon Hill), I found the message in this book not just motivational, but very real. Very real because while the author and I share very similar backgrounds, this well written roadmap for success can be applied to any life plan, career or desired state in life. The author gives the reader very simple yet profound steps to reach whatever goals you may be seeking.

I remember my first encounter with Mr. Bowers (Tim) several years ago as a young entrepreneur seeking to grow his janitorial and commercial cleaning firm. Not far removed from college, I remember quite vividly thinking "Wow....for a recent college graduate and from humble beginnings, this young man has a focus and drive not typically seen with persons his age". I was immediately drawn to him because I saw so much of myself in him. That's only part of the story.....what I've witnessed over the past five years has been remarkable as I've seen him live out *"Average to Awesome"*. What makes Mr.

Bowers road map to success so compelling is the fact that I've had a front row seat watching it unfold. In my 51 years, I'm not certain I've seen anyone at his age as focused, determined and disciplined to live a story worth telling.

I recommend this book to any and all. It is very timely because there is a need today for a message of hope for all but particularly youth including high school and college students. It wasn't until my late twenties that I became familiar with the aforementioned authors Schwartz and Kimbro, and I can only imagine where I would be had I not read a road map for success such as this book. The simple notion of "Failing to plan is planning to fail" was so profound that it ignited the fire to not allow myself to become complacent.

Tim allows the reader to walk the road map of his life in autobiographical fashion while allowing a message of hope, resiliency and success. While there were many statements that spoke to my inner spirit, his statement "Your success is not only attached to a process but it's attached to many sacrifices" spoke volumes to me.

While Schwartz and Kimbro's books were timely at a critical point in my life, Tim's road map reminded me that Average *to Awesome* is a lifelong process. I thank God for the blessing of not only knowing him but the maturity to learn from someone who was an infant when I read my first motivational book!

Darrin T. Thomas

President

Thomas Media Group, LLC

SC Black Pages and Black Expo

INTRODUCTION

Dear reader,

I DID IT! You may be wondering why I am so excited. The reason is I've talked about writing a book over a year ago and now it's finally finished! You may not be as enthusiastic as I am, but if you were considered an at- risk youth less likely to make it, grew up in a rural poverty-stricken area, high school was the education ceiling in your family, father was absent the majority of your life and against all odds you became a first-generation college graduate, entrepreneur, public speaker and now author, you would be elated about this milestone reached too! First thing, it doesn't matter where you come from or the circumstances you face, you can still succeed. Believe in your mind that you can do it and watch your actions produce the results you want.

In order to go from average to awesome or transition from where you are to where you want to be, you must first understand there's a process involved, process meaning over time, not overnight. Don't give your dreams a microwave timeframe. Allow what you truly want to develop, grow and sprout. There are levels to success and you won't get to the level you desire until you excel where you are currently. That's how you have to think. Therefore, enjoy the process along the way for it's going to teach and prepare you for the next level once you complete this one.

Endure the process! Whatever it is you desire in life to attain whether it's your high school diploma, college degree, master's degree, PhD, becoming a professional athlete or owning your business, you must be prepared to outlast the arduous times along the way. I wish I could tell you it's going to be easy, but anything worth having is worth working hard to achieve. Anything worth having is possible to the person that has faith. Anything worth having is possible to the person that never gives up. Anything worth having is possible to the person that confidently believes they can do it. Anything worth having is possible to the person that's bold, relentless and fearless towards what they want in life. To be honest, I never in my wildest dreams thought I would become an author. NEVER! However, I utter the words of the great Nelson Mandela, *"It always seems impossible until it's done."* I believe what you think you can't do is merely a thought waiting on you to prove it wrong.

My inspiration to write this book came from my passion of wanting to help the youth, students and young adults in my hometown community and around the world beat the odds to reach their level of success. Let's go through this process together reaching new heights to create the life you are striving to bring into fruition! Use this book as your dream or goal GPS system to break barriers and navigate through the process to success. My hopes are after you read this book, you're going to be transformed, inspired and motivated to not only go from average to awesome, but to take action towards making the impossible, POSSIBLE!

Let's make it happen!

Tim Bowers

Average to Awesome Agreement

Time to begin!

Let me start off by saying "thanks-a-million" for picking up my book. I truly appreciate the support and love. This book is for YOU! What goals, dreams or ideas are you telling yourself are impossible to do? Think about that someone, somewhere counting on you to become a college graduate, get that huge promotion, become a doctor or open that business. This book denounces the mindset of "I can't" and helps shift your thinking to "I can." It's not impossible for you to do; you've just told yourself too long it is. Are you ready to do the unthinkable?

Before we move forward, I need your commitment and signature.

I, ____________________ will commit to the process, work hard and give my best effort every day to assure my goals, ideas and dreams become a reality.

Here are my expectations for you:

1. Take your time reading each chapter and take notes.
2. Answer each question honestly after each chapter and use those answers to help you finish your process.
3. Share your favorite chapter(s), quotes and what you learned from this book on social media using hashtag #averagetoawesome

Okay, enough with the small talk......Let's START!

Chapter 1

Lose the Average Mentality

You are today where your thoughts have brought you. You will be tomorrow where your thoughts take you.

-James Allen

Before you can transition from average to awesome you must understand nothing will change in your life until your mindset changes first. If you think where you are is where you will always be, you're living with an average mentality. This mindset is dangerous and can persuade you to think what you're trying to achieve is impossible. You become satisfied with giving "JUST ENOUGH" to get by. You become content with the results received. You have no eagerness to do more than what you're already doing. Is this you my friend? I hope not, but if so, it's time to lose that average mentality. If you are a student or a working professional, this mediocre way of thinking is not going to improve your academic performance or make you a stand-out person for any promotion. Escape from this mindset, put forth more effort towards what you want and watch how your life and results start to change. Success begins in the mind and shows itself in your results. An average mentality will yield you an average life.

Every goal you set will require a different level of thinking to execute. If you don't transform your mind-set, next level achievements become difficult to accomplish. The reason is average mentality confines you to limits, small thinking and complacency. You start to believe there's only so far you can go or so much you can attain. When in actuality there's no shortage of possibilities or opportunities in this world, just people's inability to think outside of the box. That's why it's imperative to know that the mindset that got you where you are today will not be enough to get you where you want to be tomorrow.

During a motivational classroom session at A.C. Flora High School, I shared with an audience of 12-15 students the disappointment I received at the end of my high school sophomore year. My grade point average dropped from a 3.4 my freshman year to a 2.9 by the completion of my sophomore year. WOW! The look on their faces said, "How Tim?" In my 9th grade year, I was more focused driven with a mindset of excelling in every class. However, once my 10th grade year started, I accepted having an average mentality. School was not a priority to me and my grades dropped because of it. My mindset was geared towards chasing girls, hanging out late and doing just enough to pass each class. After I received my grades, I became displeased over my lack of effort shown that year. I lost sight of "WHY" I needed to do well in school, graduate and go to college. As a high school student, I didn't realize how much was riding on me to change the history in my family. The education level in my household stopped at high school. I needed to break the glass ceiling but if my mindset and work ethic didn't change, my GPA would continue to plummet and the education cycle in my family would continue.

To explain this fact to my audience I used a money mindset example to show when change is necessary your mentality has to shift. I had my high school students raise their hands if they knew how to make $50 (all hands raised), $100 (all hands raised), $500 (some hands raised), $1,000 (very few hands raised) $10,000 (no hands raised), $50,000 (no hands raised). They gave me that, "STOP PLAYING" look when I asked them to raise their hands for $10,000 and $50,000. Afterwards, I shared with them a golden nugget that I believed resonated with them: "You can't use the same $50 mindset to make $50,000." My point was, what I did to make the 2.9, couldn't be the same mindset I would apply to increase my GPA to a 3.0 or better. You will get different results once you start changing the way you think and improve your work ethic. I know this to be true because at the end of my junior year at Allendale-Fairfax High School, my GPA increased to a 3.1! The hardest thing for someone to do who has an average mentality is make an intentional decision to change their mindset.

Average doesn't mean you're a failure or a terrible person; it just means you have some work to do!

How to Lose the Average Mentality?

Work on Your Mind

It's said that the best project you can ever work on is YOU! I believe a major part of that development is your mindset. You must challenge and recondition your mind every day to think beyond the limitation you've set for yourself. Make reading, learning something new daily and consuming positivity a priority and not "when I feel like doing it." Think about it this way, your mind has plenty of seeds planted (ideas, visions, dreams and goals). If you don't water your mind as often, how do you expect your seedlings to grow? Always know your thoughts are controlled by you; why not use them to your advantage? If you can contemplate to yourself the reasons why something won't work or can't be done, you can also tell yourself the reasons why it will. You have that kind of power to shift your thinking instantly. I agree with the United Negro College Fund's famous slogan, "A Mind is a Terrible Thing to Waste," for whatever the mind focuses on long enough, the body will eventually take action to achieve it. If your thoughts are constantly on finding ways to change your life, the change you seek will eventually become your reality.

A CALL OF ACTION

What can you do to start working on changing your mindset?

____

____

____

____

Change the Company You Keep

A statement you should always remember is, "Everyone can't go where God is trying to take you." Many people are frustrated on their journey because they're trying to shift their thinking and take average people with them on their path to success. Spending too much time with average people is going to make everything you're going after very difficult to accomplish. Be intentional with who you allow to consume your time. Don't just amass friends just to say you have plenty. Connect with like-minded individuals who are movers and shakers working to become successful. Find people who are winning in life and ask them how they are doing it. The average mentality of others will keep you from stepping into your greatness, but the moment you make a deliberate decision to change your association, you become attractive to success. Always remember the people around you mostly have or will influence you in some way. The question you have to ask yourself, "Is having them in my circle helping or hurting me?"

Take the Limits Off

Many people limit themselves and remain average because of self-doubt. What it does is make you question or hesitate on taking action towards what you want. To combat against that, you have to quiet the negative self-talk by speaking out loud declaring, I WILL WIN! I CAN DO THIS! IT IS POSSIBLE! I HAVE NO LIMITS! Don't allow self-doubt to convince you to settle for being average. What people don't realize is thinking creates ideas. With those ideas you can build, invent, produce or start new trends. With one idea, you can create a new world for yourself.

When I think about my childhood, I must be transparent that there were many limitations. One of which was not having my father to guide me from a young boy to man. He was a drug addict and his focus was not on giving me any guidance. However, my mindset was against all odds, I was still going to succeed. That mentality helped me become who I am today. You may have to go through trial and error to achieve your goal, but don't allow what you don't have to keep you stagnate. Extraordinary doesn't happen until your expectation supersedes the comfort zone of your mindset. Take the limits off your life! Your old way of thinking, which is embedded with boundaries, is not going to give you the life you desire. Greatness awaits you once those impediments that control your mind are removed.

Average to Awesome Success Tip

You must expand your mind to reach the level of success you want. Read and study successful people to learn what they know. Make your mind an employee and give it work to do every day. Change the way you think and you will most definitely change your circumstances.

Questions to Consider

1. How am I going to use the information in this chapter to change my mindset?

___

___

___

___

2. What can I do to feed my mind in the morning before going to school or work?

___

___

___

___

3. What limitations have I given myself that I need to remove?

___

___

___

___

Chapter 2

Dream B.I.G. Set Goals. Achieve Them ALL!

"Hold fast to dreams, for if dreams die, life is a broken winged bird that cannot fly."

–Langston Hughes

Go **B.I.G.**: **B**ecome **I**nspired to reach your **G**reatness. If people think your dreams are too BIG, it's because the way they think is too small. The simple truth is if you're not excited about your dreams, you're playing small and therefore cheating yourself. This average way of thinking limits the possibility of you reaching your fullest potential. Nothing great ever came to a person who dreamed or thought small. Those who are intentional about making the desires of their heart a priority will eventually achieve greatness.

To dream B.I.G. and not set goals or have a plan of action means you're not serious about making that dream a reality. You need a plan, something you intend to do. The plan has to have goals to move you closer to your mark every time a specific task is achieved. Every accomplished goal measures your progress. Then, you need to develop a strategy to execute the plan. These are creative ways to navigate you to your destination. This blueprint you create will be considered your Dream B.I.G. GPS. This will give you a visual of how you will do it, help you understand what you have to do along the way, and gives you a plan of action to follow.

My Challenge to YOU

Right now, take the time to think about what your dream is and write it down. Afterwards, create a plan, set some goals and develop a strategy to execute!

What's my DREAM?

____

____

What's my PLAN?

____

____

____

____

What goals do I need to set in order to make my dream a reality?

Goal #1

____

____

Goal #2

____

____

Goal #3

____

____

What's my STRATEGY?

____

____

____

____

Make sure you schedule time to work on your dreams, whether that's in the morning, evening, after school or work. Develop a log that prioritize and tracks your hours of grinding daily. This creates a weekly and monthly progress report to help you measure and monitor your effort towards the goal you set.

SEE EXAMPLE ON THE NEXT PAGE

USE THE EXAMPLE BELOW TO SCHEDULE TIME BLOCKS

AVERAGE TO AWESOME
Daily Grind Sheet

DAILY PRIORITY LIST:
A list of the most important work you need to be doing daily.

DAILY TIME MANAGEMENT LIST:
The way you use and organize your time daily.

DAY: Saturday
DATE: January 8th

Priority 1:
Research Colleges & Universities
Time blocked: 8:00am-9:30am

Priority 2:

____

Time blocked:

Priority 3:

____

Time blocked:

Total Daily Grind: 1 hour, 30 mins

What's most important to understand about this exercise is you MUST be honest with yourself. How much time are you willing to devote to your goals and dreams each day? You're reading this book because I took a BIG dream and made it a reality. If your dream or goal matters, stay determined, disciplined, persistent and consistent every step of the way during the process (Read more about process in chapter 3). Use this blueprint to help you get started on your journey.

When you read success stories about how Walt Disney, Oprah Winfrey, Bill Gates, Tyler Perry, the Wright Brothers and J.K. Rowling became successful, you learn it all began with an idea or dream that eventually manifested into greatness. They had dreams to do the unthinkable and regardless of what people said about their plans, they never gave up or stopped trying. What you can learn from these pioneers is you can't go from average to awesome without a dream or goal to go after. The key is to understand success doesn't happen by mistake; it happens when you intentionally take action and remain focused on the work not the dream (chapter 6 explains this concept more in detail).

One of my favorite hobbies is watching movies. The best feeling is having a great movie to watch, some good food, an ice-cold drink (lemonade), a cozy seat and no interruptions. That's a day of relaxation for me. However, while writing this book, I had to give up hours of sleep and my favorite hobby for many days. While others were in the bed before 12:00am I was up writing to 3:00 a.m., sometimes 4:00 a.m. in the morning. What you must always understand is never glorify someone's chapter 20 without knowing what it took for them to reach that milestone. Your success is not only attached to a process, but it's also attached to many sacrifices. Many of us don't want to go through anything to have everything.

Don't Let People Talk You Out of It

I grew up in a rural area, Allendale County, South Carolina, where you had to be creative to have fun. On Saturdays, my brother John and I along with some friends from around town would play tackle football with no pads on in a field behind a church. Once everyone made it to the field, two people had to be team captain and pick who they wanted on their team. My brother was always picked because he could throw the ball. He loved the all-time great Dan Marino who played for the Miami Dolphins. I was one of the young boys along with several others who got picked last, but we were still on a team. My favorite player was Jerry Rice who played for the San

Francisco 49ers. I would line up in my wide receiver position on offense and run routes thinking I was Jerry Rice hardly ever dropping a ball thrown to me. We would play for hours running up and down the field. Everyone that came out was competitive, but you could tell who had the potential to be great. Most people didn't know John really liked football, the quarterback position in particular. So much so, he thought he was worthy to play for our high school football team at the quarterback position. John eventually tried out for the team and performed pretty well, but he quit before the coaches had time to work on his skill. John allowed his goal to be tampered with by other people's negative opinion about his ability to play the game. When people doubt you, don't become discouraged. Let your actions speak louder than your words. The moment you decide to not be defeated by any opposition, you become the master of your fate.

Make the Impossible, Possible

In order to do the unthinkable, you must not give in to the notion that it's impossible. You must understand IMPOSSIBLE is just a big word. What you say you can't do is merely an opinion not a fact. The words you speak and thoughts you think have power to create the life you want or destroy your chances of having the life you desire. Whenever you make a decision to do something out of the norm there's always going to be a flood of “what if” thoughts and people’s opinions. Neither are helpful and can keep you from taking action. Les Brown said it best, “*Other people’s opinion of you does not have to become your reality.*” Understand on the journey to make your dreams become a reality there’s the N.P.E (Negative Pull Effect) and the P.P.E (Positive Pull Effect). These effects are pulling you like a tug-a-war game whenever you’re working to make the impossible possible.

NEGATIVE
PULL EFFECT

PEOPLE'S OPINIONS -
What you're aiming for is impossible

NEGATIVE SELF TALK -
I can't do that

HATERS & DOUBTERS-
You're going to fail

Don't give up! Hard work pays off.

POSITIVE
PULL EFFECT

POSITIVE FRIENDS-
That's a great idea go for it

A STRONG SUPPORT GROUP-
Go after what you believe in

POSITIVE THINKING-
Believe as though anything is possible

The pull effect you feed is the one that's going to make your decision. In the contest of tug-of-war each side has a team of people trying to pull the opposite side across their winning line. The game is competitive with certain people positioned in the front and back. When the game starts, each side pulls with all their strength and might. They go back and forth until one side gives in, giving momentum to the other group to win. The team that wins understands only the strong survives! Your positive pull effect has to be more powerful than the negative pull effect to achieve the goals you set. Making the impossible possible is going to require you to starve and block out all negativity on your journey to success. It's not easy. That's why thinking positive, having positive friends and surrounding yourself with a strong support group keeps negativity from winning.

Five Powerful Ways to Make the Impossible, Possible

1. **Have a made-up mind-** This is when you're convinced with an unwavering attitude you can do it without the slightest doubt.
2. **Shift your thinking-** The thoughts that you allow to imprison your dreams can sabotage your future.
3. **Have a plan of action-** This is when you have a crystal-clear vision of what you want and how you're going to get it.
4. **Lean on your WHY-**It's those things you've identified in your life that will keep you from quitting on yourself and your dreams. It's those reasons that remind you why you have to make the impossible, possible.
5. **Understand it's a process**-Success does not happen overnight. You have to endure the journey to reap the reward.

Average to Awesome Success Tip

You have to be the first person to believe your dream can come true. Never let anyone make you believe your dream is impossible. Use their doubt as motivation to prove them wrong!

Questions to consider

1. What excites me the most about my goals and aspirations?

____

____

____

____

2. Who are the people I can ask for help, direction or guidance when I'm faced with a challenge, I believe is impossible?

____

____

____

____

3. What will the attainment of the goal or dream do for me?

____

____

____

____

Chapter 3

Overtime Not Overnight

"Never give up on a dream just because of the time it will take to accomplish it."

-Earl Nightingale

It was Maya Angelou who said, *"All great achievements require time."* That time points to one word, process. Whenever you make a decision to embark upon a journey to enter college, start working a job or entrepreneurship, the reward or success doesn't come right away. It takes time! Don't become impatient or stressed because the goal you're trying to achieve is taking too long. Process is defined as a series of actions or steps taken in order to achieve a particular end. You have to understand anything worth having is worth the wait. A beautiful flower doesn't bloom overnight nor does an apple tree bear fruit in one day. Your goals and dreams must be viewed from the same perspective.

Success doesn't happen when you want it to; that's why it's called a process. Look at the timeline or beginning photos of your favorite artist, athlete or entrepreneur via Instagram or Facebook. As you start to move through their page looking at where they started and where they are now, you see progression. The picture quality even looks different as you scroll through their profile. The individuals knew if they were going to achieve their set goal, quitting or staying stuck wasn't an option. If you work hard with your head down and feet moving, by the time you look up, the finish line will be within arm's reach. Strive for progress and know it doesn't matter how you start; it only matters how you finish.

Take Kevin Hart for example. He will go down arguably as one of the best comedians and entertainers who ever held a microphone on stage. Do you remember him playing in the movie *Soul Plane*? The movie was funny. He was one of the main actors, but it definitely wasn't his best performance. He had to develop into the superstar he is today. Now, Kevin is selling out football stadiums. His movies are box office hits across the world bringing in millions of dollars in my Kevin Hart voice, "Yep, that's a lot of zeros". How did he go from average to awesome? He never abandoned his process. He stayed the course and grinded his way to the top. If the reward you're going after requires you to do extra, stay longer, grind for a certain number of years, it would behoove you to not rush your matriculation to satisfy your lack of patience.

Lose the Microwave Mindset

In an age of quick fixes, instant gratification and get-rich-quick schemes, there is a misconception that you can have what you want without doing much work. The simple truth is you have to give what you're working on time to develop and grow. How long does it take a baby to turn 21? Exactly! It takes 21 years to be 21, there's no way around it. What people miss about the importance of a process is growth happens in the moment someone decides not to cut corners but embrace their process. The pain is never long lasting. You have to trust the journey and endure to the end. If success was easy to attain, everyone would be successful, but the reality is people don't enjoy working for the goal they've set. That's why shortcuts are searched through Google every day. What people fail to realize, especially our next generation, is the amount of time and energy spent looking for easy paths could have been spent working on strategies to accomplish both their goals and dreams.

Although all goals don't need years to accomplish, there are aspirations that require extensive time to receive the reward. What I've learned from my childhood struggles to creating new history in my family is that you can't jump from average to awesome. You can only progress to that level of success. I had to complete 16 years of school to become a first-generation college graduate. There was an elementary, middle and high school level to complete. Then, I had to do another four years in college. If you think about it from that standpoint, you will understand the words I shared in the beginning of this chapter by Maya Angelou, *"All great achievements require time."*

Take Thanksgiving for example, the immediate family and loved ones traveling expect the food to be well seasoned, cooked, some made from scratch and the desserts baked to perfection. The family members cooking understand everything on the menu takes time to finish. The process can't be rushed if they want the food to be cooked right. Therefore, the family that's traveling is not too concerned about the wait because the delay is well worth it. I believe if you grind without the mindset of quick, fast and in a hurry, you place yourself in the best position to succeed and sustain your success.

Trust Your Process

After leaving my job with Wells Fargo to take a position with Thomas Media Group, I had accumulated close to $10,000 in my savings. Keep in mind at Wells Fargo, I was guaranteed a paycheck bi-weekly. However, my transition to TMG was different. The company started me off with full commission pay. If you're not familiar with the term "commission" it simply means if you don't close sales, you don't get paid. What I didn't factor was the length of time it would take me to start making money. In my sales training and seeing other sales reps present sales presentations, I confidently thought my role as an Account Executive (Sales Rep) wouldn't be hard. Boy, was I WRONG! It took me 5-6 months to close my first sale. Would you have stayed on your job if you didn't receive a steady paycheck for that length of time? Probably not! I understand but take this golden nugget, don't jump ship when your process is not going as planned. It's the test that produces the testimony!

During my "no commission – pay" period, I had to rely on my savings to pay the bills. There were plenty of nights I questioned my decision leaving Wells Fargo as I'm sure you have already assumed. My money was depleting fast and bill collectors didn't feel any remorse. Their hands were always out every month collecting payments. I contemplated many times leaving Thomas Media Group, but the determination in me wouldn't allow me to do it. There was an inner fighter in me that didn't permit me to give up. YES, that process was rough and there were thoughts of quitting at least 3-4 times a week. Even after I started to attain some success there were still times I struggled to close sales. My personal account at one point showed $1 and some change. I had to ask family and friends for money to pay some of my monthly bills. I was embarrassed but it fueled me to grind harder. If you believe in what you're doing, trust your process.

It took me two and a half years to really start seeing real success in my Account Executive position. That's when sales took a turn upward. Out of nowhere during that time I was receiving sale inquiries to close deals and my commission pay rose tremendously and consistently for quite some time. My closed sales were not only small businesses, but a great mixture of corporate clients which yielded a larger commission payout.

If I had to pinpoint one contributor to my success, especially my financial increase, I would have to say it was my commitment to tithing. Even when I wasn't making much money, I still tithe, which is giving 10% of what you earn back to God through church. This book is not about religion or to persuade you in any way. I'm simply conveying what I believed helped change my financial hardship during my process. My financial success during that time allowed me to increase my tithing amount, loan money to family members who were in need and deposit money to build my savings account from the bottom. That experience taught me life doesn't always go as planned. However, when you trust your process, God will reward your obedience.

Endure NOW to ENJOY later

Sometimes it's hard to watch friends and family have fun on weekends, celebrate holidays and travel. Your life right now may consist of working on a class assignment, job project, studying for a major test, practicing on your craft or trying to finish writing a book. Just so you know, you're not a loser and I encourage you to work while you wait. No one knows when your breakthrough will occur, but if you quit, you will never know either. Stay passionate towards the pursuit of your dreams. You have no control over life's time clock, but what you can control is the amount of sweat equity you deposit into your goals and aspirations daily. It may be difficult now, but think about what your life will be like once you receive that degree, pay raise, promotion, acceptance letter to start your masters or doctorate program or that opportunity to vacation wherever you like. Anything is possible to the person that believes. Your job is to keep grinding, hustling and working hard every day to transition from where you are to where you want to be. #averagetoawesome

Average to Awesome Success Tip

To finish strong, you have to obey your process with the understanding of overtime not overnight.

The idea is to learn while you work and be patient while you wait. You're running a marathon not a sprint.

Questions to Consider

1. What can I start doing now to take my grind in school or at work to another level?

____

____

____

____

2. What are some changes I need to make to stay focus on finishing my goals?

____

____

____

____

3. What can I do to assure I will not quit when the process becomes tough?

____

____

____

____

Chapter 4

Feel the Fear and Do It Anyway

"In my opinion, the only person worse than a quitter is the person afraid to begin."

– John Maxwell

Imagine for a moment what your life will be like once you have reached your pre-determined level of success. Everything you have dreamed, envisioned and worked for came true. You received that undergraduate degree; you landed a position at your dream job; you cut the ribbon to that business you always envisioned; you joined the millionaire club; you traveled the world with no worries visiting blue water oceans, five-star resorts and white sandy beaches. What a great feeling! What a great life! Now, rewind those thoughts to the beginning before all the success. Imagine yourself with the potential to make your dreams a reality but you were too fearful of the unknown to start the journey. What fears are you giving permission to withhold you from having the desires of your heart?

Don't Let Fear Decide Your Future

Everyone experiences fear; however, some realize sooner than later that what they are afraid of is nothing but False Evidence Appearing Real. It's a negative tactic of the mind that fights to paralyze you from starting any process to achievement. The mind is so powerful that if it succeeds in stalling you long enough from taking action: your vision, your dreams and your goals will never have a chance to manifest. I encourage you to fight back against any adversary trying to plague your mind to believe you can't do it. What if some of our great leaders of the past and present allowed fear to stop them from fulfilling their purpose? How different do you think life would be today? What is something you wanted to do but because of fear you talked your way out of it?

Write down the desires of your heart.

____

____

____

____

Write down your fears.

____

____

____

____

Write down on each line: DO IT ANYWAY!

____

____

____

____

Here's a secret: if you wait to start you may never do it because life will never give you a perfect time to take action. What you are afraid of doing is not going anywhere and will remain present until you face it. You have the capability right now to change your situation for the better and remove the boundaries stopping you from doing the unthinkable. Take the first step! Start by listening and being more attentive in class. Start by applying for school and researching scholarships. Start by beginning the application process for the job. Start by coming in to work 30 minutes earlier and leaving 30 minutes later to show your boss you really want that promotion. Start by researching and studying successful people who are doing what you want to do in life. Start the process and don't focus on the imperfections of your first move. When you make this decision, you are conquering the fear holding you back and building self-confidence to continue pressing forward!

Turn Fear into Motivation

One of my nicknames in my household as a teenager was "banker." I received this name because I always had a dollar when no one else had one. I learned the concept of "working for what you want" at an early age because my mom struggled tremendously as a single parent trying to provide for me as well as my younger brothers and sisters. I was born into a low-income family, living mostly in a mobile home. I saw my mom struggle year after year trying to purchase school clothes, shoes, and supplies, pay the rent and keep food on the table. I wanted to take some of the pressure off of my mom because her finances were fixed every month from the government. Therefore, I found a job to save and make my own money. My first job was at a convenient store and meat market as a stock boy getting paid "under the table", which meant no checks issued; I was paid cash. I worked 3-5 days a week and was paid weekly. The money I made afforded me the opportunity to save, purchase my own school clothes, shoes and supplies. The majority of everything I needed from 9th - 12th grade was paid out of my pocket. My fear as a young teenager was my mom not being able to buy me whatever I needed for school every year. That fear forced me to find work, but the experience showed me that I didn't want a life where I was relying on someone else. I wanted to be in control of my destiny. That's why my pursuit of success was a necessity.

I learned that to turn fear into motivation, you must have a burning desire to succeed, strong confidence in yourself and a fearless attitude. That's how I was able to provide for myself as a high school student and beyond. Fear must become your footstool not your prison. Draw your motivation from making the desire to succeed greater than what you fear. Don't be fearful, BE FEARLESS!

Most people lose the battle with fear because they are indecisive on what they want in life. When you confidently know what you want your mind doesn't easily fall for fear traps. I believe the emotion of fear is inevitable, but you don't have to allow it to control you. Nothing can stop you unless you give it permission. When you're scared to do something, see it as a challenging force pushing you to step outside of your comfort zone.

Everything You Want is On the Other Side of Fear

Do what scares you!

Whenever shifts or changes are about to happen in your life, fear is always present. In any process of transition, the unknown frightens people. The doubts, what-ifs and fears paralyze people from moving forward. You need to have enough courage to take the risk anyway.

The idea of speaking publicly came into fruition in 2013 after leaving my full-time job with Wells Fargo to pursue a sales career with Thomas Media Group. This unorthodox move was frowned upon by many because it meant that I had to leave my job security, health benefits, 401k investment and the possibility of moving up the corporate ladder. I must admit, it was an intimidating transition. My new job didn't offer the same benefits as Wells Fargo and I wasn't guaranteed a paycheck. I remember crying as I was leaving the parking lot of Wells Fargo, wondering if I had made a mistake. I was driving down Interstate 20 West asking God for his guidance with this transition. Even though I had a plan, I knew His plan was far greater than my own.

The added value of moving into this new position was the chance to network with different professionals and to create my own work schedule. The flexibility allowed me to cultivate a passion for speaking. In my position as an AccountExecutive, I delivered sales presentations, showing business owners how my product could help promote their company across the state of South Carolina. I really enjoyed it and thought, "What if I could do this more often for different schools and businesses?" That's when I started researching different types of speakers who were successful with motivational speaking. I saw how they changed lives through telling their life story and I wanted to do the same. Eventually, my passion for speaking helped me find my purpose to empower youth, students and millennials across the world on how to move from "Average to Awesome."

It was several months after I made the decision to change careers when I was given the opportunity to speak to several groups of high school students for their career day which kicked off my journey. I remember being very nervous but excited to share a message that was crafted to motivate, inspire and empower students, but also teachers, faculty and staff. After I spoke, a Student Government Association (SGA) representative asked if I would be interested in serving as their guest speaker for a leadership rally. In addition, I was requested by the school counselor to speak to their incoming freshman class of over 100 students! Later, I was requested by one of the teachers to speak to her class of 12 students who didn't believe it was possible for them to succeed in life. After speaking to that class there was a written article featured on their website raving about the message I shared on ***"Key Principles for Accomplishing Any Goal."*** Those key principles were: Believe it's Possible. Be Determined. Be Persistent. Here's a testimony from the teacher who brought me in to speak to her students:

"Thank You" just does not seem adequate enough to convey how I feel about the presentation you gave to my language lab students at Mid-Carolina High School. Since delivering the "Key Principles for Accomplishing Any Goal", I

have had many students to comment on how your speech changed their outlook on life. You are the person who exposed them to the idea of pursing success by identifying goals, making better choices, and continuing in spite of difficulties. Once again, the knowledge, information, and enthusiasm you shared really had an impact on my students—you left them yearning for a better tomorrow.

I realized after those engagements, my decision to leave Wells Fargo was the turning point of my life. You must get through your fears to reach the person you're working to become.

Average to Awesome Success Tip

Feel the fear and pursue your goals and dreams anyway!

Questions to Consider

1. What fears do I need to face in order for me to go from average to awesome?

____

____

____

____

2. What reasons do I have to turn my fears into motivation?

____

____

____

____

3. What future regrets would I have if I continue to allow fear to control my decisions?

____

____

____

____

Chapter 5

No One Said It Would Be Easy

"If you want something you never had, you must be willing to do something you never done."

–Thomas Jefferson

In the game of boxing, a fighter has a ten-count to get back on their feet when knocked down. Once the boxer rises to their feet from the canvas, the referee examines the fighter to make sure they are stable enough to continue. If the boxer is not, the referee waves their hands to indicate the fight is over. If the boxer shows readiness to go forward, the referee makes the judgment to allow the fighter to continue. What is important to understand about the boxer who's been knocked down is there's always a choice to either get up or stay down. In moments that appear to be defeat, you must choose whether to get up and keep fighting or stay down and give up the possibility of becoming who you're striving to be. YOU decide!

Go 12 Rounds

All boxers train and prepare for months before entering the ring to fight their opponent. The fighters understand the importance of eating right, self-discipline and staying consistent with their daily workout routines. I can imagine that on some days their body screams take a break, but their mind yells there's no room for breaks, especially when you don't know when the next opportunity will arrive. All you have is now! Therefore, every chance you get to work on your goals and dreams, you must give 110% and nothing less. This life is designed to reveal every thought, vision, and goal or dream you have inside of you. If you decide not to go 12 rounds and check out during the sixth, think about who would be affected by your decision. You fighting to the end not only benefits you, but it inspires others to fight for their future too.

The fight is never easy, but it's worth it. Winning takes grit, a relentless attitude and determination from you to finish strong. When you put forth more daily effort and grind consistently towards your goals and aspirations, you will eventually succeed. The moment you lose hope in yourself you forfeit the opportunity to become successful. Believe through the odds, through the pain and through the setbacks that you will still come out victorious. Everyone will not understand the choices you make to achieve your goals and that's OKAY. Don't spend valuable time trying to convince people to believe in your vision. What God has for your life can be too much for people who think small. Never forget that the vision, dream or idea was given to you, not them.

Not everyone has the heart to fight for what they want. In fact, some people quit before their breakthrough because they don't have enough courage to stand tall in the midst of difficult times. If you expect to reach greatness you must endure every storm your journey encounters. The adversity along the way is a part of the process. When the path to success becomes tough that's when true champions come alive. The weak will quit! Only the strong will thrive! Which one are you? Are you willing to fight for the person you're trying to become?

Tough Times Never Last

At the age of 27 in 2014, I experienced a rough financial period in my life. I was still working in sales and lived mostly off commission and a small salary. If you know anything about the sales industry, then you understand it's not for the weak hearted. At my company, the peak period of closing the most sales were the first and fourth quarter of the year. That means January to March 31st and October to December 31st. During these times I had to plan accordingly, follow up promptly and be assertive to ensure I met my personal goal as well as the company goal. It was the fourth quarter and I had all my prospects and potential clients to close over $35,000 in sales. I was sure of it....at least I thought.

My daily activities were catered to new and current advertisers to renew their contract. Those tasks consisted of: calling, sending e-mails, following up, setting appointments, searching for new sales leads and driving around to knock on doors. However, even with all my efforts and hard work I still wasn't closing the amount of sales weekly, to hit my numbers monthly. Most of the business owners I presented my product to didn't want to buy. You can imagine my frustration at this point because nothing was working in my favor. As the sales period and year came to an end, I was faced with the reality of not meeting my personal or company goal. My sales for that quarter didn't exceed $10,000. I was devastated because some of my monthly bills went unpaid; my car insurance lapsed and I barely had the money to pay my rent at the beginning of each month. The struggle was REAL!

What I had to learn in that period of my life was embrace the struggle, but don't stop grinding. Neither my work ethic nor my mindset changed. By the time my next sales period ended (1st quarter 2015), I was able to pay all my monthly bills on time and place insurance back on my car. In life you may bend, but don't break! So often in the pursuit of success you will have to go through, to get through. Those moments will test you mentally, emotionally and financially, but you must stay the course. Even when you've studied, prepared and prayed, issues are still prone to happen. So how do you handle difficult times? You have to look at them the same way you do cuts and bruises- they will heal eventually. Robert Schuller said it this way, *"Tough times never last, but tough people do."*

Winners Find Ways to Win

There is a quote I love that was written by author Napoleon Hill, *"A quitter never wins-and-a winner never quits."*

I believe most people lose in life because they mentally count themselves out too early. Point your finger towards your mind and repeat, "I must win here first, before I can have any victory in life." You must think like a winner in order to be one. The Book of Proverbs (23:7) states, "As a man thinketh in his heart so is he."

Think Like a Winner:

I believe in myself!

I win before I start!

I am a champion!

I am the master of my fate!

I am the head not the tail!

I CAN succeed! I WILL succeed! I MUST succeed!

I believe winning is just as contagious as losing. However, what winners do more than losers is focus more on the positive rather than the negative. It is not hard to see what's not going right, but when you take the time to figure out how to turn a negative into a positive you instantaneously become a winner. If you are not where you want to be right now academically, financially or career wise, channel your energy and focus on finding ways to change what you don't like. Don't think you're a loser because the turnaround hasn't happened yet. Tony Robbins said it best, "No matter how many mistakes you make or how slow you progress, you're still way ahead of everyone who isn't trying." You're a winner so find a way to win!

I believe the way you start is to create a habit of winning. This is done by building momentum in what you're doing to create a snowball effect. What happens is every day that momentum builds your confidence, and attitude builds with it. Think about this way, if a student makes enough A's on pop quizzes and classroom assignments, by the time that final test comes around, that student would have accumulated enough small victories to knock the BIG one out the park! If you treat what you want out of life in this manner, you will find a way to go from average to awesome.

Some people think or believe the process to success happens without any help. That's not true. To reach any level of achievement; it will not only require your sweat equity, but the effort of someone else too. You need the help from your teachers, professors, mentors, parents and coaches on the journey from average to awesome. A winner understands nothing great is achieved without help along the way.

Life doesn't give manuals explaining what to do with every part of it; however, there are people that can guide, direct and lead you to your destination. You just have to be willing to ask for help! When success paths are not straight or directions are not clear, don't quit. Winners find ways to win. Losers complain and make excuses. Which one are you?

Average to Awesome Success Tip

Use the pain, struggles and challenges of your life as motivation to elevate your grind.

Questions to Consider

1. What am I not doing to achieve the level of success I want in school, work or business?

____

____

____

____

2. What can I do to ensure my next move is my best move?

____

____

____

____

3. What are three ways I can keep myself motivated when I'm feeling defeated?

____

____

____

____

Chapter 6

Focus On the Work Not the Dream

"Everybody has a dream, but not everybody has a grind."

-Dr. Eric Thomas

Have you ever daydreamed about your future aspirations so long that they appeared real? You become so immersed into your imagination that you actually see what your level of success looks like. Then you snap out of it upset because reality hits you in the gut! Please don't tell me I'm the only one who has had this experience! The quickest way to escape your present and live in your future is by dreaming. You don't have to wait years to receive a degree from school or gain job experience before you're eligible to work in a particular position. You can live and travel the places you've always wanted to for FREE! The dream gives you open access to be, do and have whatever you want in life. I think this is one of the most awesome traits of being a human being. Don't you agree?

What happens with this freedom for most people is that they sleep and wallow too long in paradise. The reality is if you want what you see, you have to work for it. Your dream will show you the finish line but won't give you a step-by-step visual on what it takes to have what you see. The missing piece to the puzzle is the work involved to make it a reality. Never stop thinking about your dream, but also remember there is work involved. Once you become more deliberate about completing the work, the mental picture of your future eventually comes true.

The problem with most students and young millennials is they want massive success without traveling through "Hard Work Blvd." Everybody wants to be at the top of the mountain, but no one wants to climb. I believe the challenge lies in their inability to focus on the tasks associated with the dream. Where your focus is, your actions will follow. Any change you've ever made was a result of what you focused on. Your actions will follow the leader. Your leader is whatever the focus is. If you ever get off track on your path from average to awesome, it's because your focus has deviated from the priority.

Don't Get Lost in The Sauce

The excitement of knowing what can transpire in your life 10, 15 or 20 years from now may give you goosebumps. However, don't get lost in your aspirations. Who you are to become will remain an image in your mind or a conversation with a friend until the work involved with the dream is completed. When you have a vision, write it down, figure out the workload attached to it and execute. Always remember, no one respects a talker unless the individual is producing great results.

Take this example: If student A dream is to become a professional football player, his focus can't solely be on watching NFL players and daydreaming about playing on his favorite team someday. The student focal point has to be locked on the work it's going to take to become a pro athlete. His "work" will entail: becoming an awesome academic student, practicing every day, being consistent with workouts, making big plays during game day, learning the game of football and staying disciplined and committed to the process. If he excels on all levels during his high school and college years, student A chances of playing Monday Night Football is very possible. Why? Student A realizes if the end result of the work he completes is top-quality, his dreams are highly achievable. Success is available to all who are willing to complete the working assignments connected to their dream.

The most important factor to focusing on the work is having a breakdown of how you're going to focus.

See that breakdown on the next page:

Focus on the Work Not the Dream Blueprint

WHAT'S YOUR DREAM? THE BIG PICTURE	YOUR REASON(S) WHY	SET A TIME	WHAT ARE YOUR BARRIERS?	WHAT WORK DO YOU NEED TO FOCUS ON?
What is your dream?	What are your reasons to keep you from quitting?	How much time will it take to achieve your goal or make your dream a reality?	List what's preventing you from taking action towards your dreams.	Figure out all the work that has to be done for the dream to come true.

This "focus on the work not the dream" blueprint is geared towards helping you accomplish your dreams, set goals and specific tasks. Each aim achieved ultimately moves you closer to the big picture, a visualization of your future self. This method helps you identify: your dream, your goals, your reasons why, your time frame to complete a task, barriers stopping your progress and your focused work.

Having a clear picture eliminates leaving success to chance and puts the focus on the work at hand. It's imperative when working to know why you're doing it. If you can't connect with your why, you risk giving up before finding the diamonds. Once you have pinpointed a time frame, you have agreed to a commitment. Don't cheat yourself in the process. Seek an accountability partner. When you become a master at not allowing difficult situations, obstacles or challenges detour your focus, you're better prepared to finish the race. In Ecclesiastes 9:11 it states, *"The race is not given to the swift nor the strong but he who endures until the end."* You must identify your barriers to eradicate those walls: procrastination, doubt, fear, other people's opinion, not enough resources, negative company, negative self-talk, excuses or poor work ethic. Once you know what's keeping you from moving forward, take the necessary action to change. In all, your "focused work" encompasses your dream(s) workload. When you know what to do, it becomes easier charting the course to your destiny.

Hard Work Pays Off

Muhammad Ali stated, "I hated every minute of training, but I said, 'Don't quit. Suffer now and live the rest of your life as a Champion."

I had a similar mindset as a teenager having to walk to work because no one in my household had a car. From my house to my job was less than a mile, but the walk appeared to be longer especially during the summers. In my small town, there weren't many places to work, but I managed to become an employee at our local Subway. In my role, I was considered a sandwich artist with a specialty in making salads. Well, not really a specialty, I was just confident that my salads were the best! I took pride in my work. On my days to clock in, I walked down Main Street from my house in my full Subway uniform: black subway hat, green Subway polo shirt, khaki pants, black shoes and my black apron in my pocket thinking, "It won't always be like this. I just have to keep working hard to save my money to buy my first car someday."

That mindset and work ethic stayed with me through college. In my junior year, I purchased my first car, a silver Mazda 626 LX for $2,700 cash at an auction. I managed to save that amount of money by doing work study consistently every year, working at a nearby grocery store, and working as a student mentor for Benedict

College's Summer Youth Leadership Institute. I also received some assistance from my father. I called my first car Lucille after my mom. That car was a thing of beauty, clean on the outside and the inside well kept. To me, that car was a symbol of what can happen if you work hard on your goals. The principle I learned from that experience taught me that anything you set your mind to can be achieved. You just have to be "Built Ford Tough" to endure the wait.

Five ways to become "Built Ford Tough":

1. Have patience.
2. Be courageous.
3. Have faith.
4. Have confidence in yourself.
5. Develop a mindset to never give up no matter how tough it gets.

The goal is to work hard and play later. I believe the enjoyment of life is much sweeter when you know you've earned the right to celebrate. Let people sleep while you grind. Let them hate while you hustle. The hard work will pay off soon enough. Every day you wake up, you're the pen and life is your paper. Don't take that power you have lightly.

Average to Awesome Success Tip

Success not only requires work but it also requires patience. What you believe you should have or be in life is not going to happen on your time. Focus on the work. Make it your priority.

Questions to Consider

1. If I started to focus more on the work and not the dream, what goal can I achieve in the next 21 days?

____

____

____

____

2. What's the work required to accomplish the dream or goal I've set?

____

____

____

____

3. What steps can I take to break the barriers that are holding me back from taking action towards my goals and dreams?

____

____

____

____

Chapter 7

The Power of Persistence

"Failure cannot cope with persistence."

–Napoleon Hill

The major goal for many college students is to secure a job prior to graduation. This was definitely my mindset as a college student. I searched, applied and interviewed with several job recruiters during my final year in school. However, some of the companies were not hiring, others I didn't get interviews for and the few jobs I did interview for, I didn't do well enough to get the position. One of the lengthy hiring processes I remember before graduation was with Wachovia Bank, now Wells Fargo for a Credit Manager position. I went through three intense interviews and traveled out of the city to complete the last one. I experienced interview fatigue and exhaustion during that process, but I was confident I would get the position.

Once I finished all three interviews, my next step was to wait on the job recruiter to decide whether I was hired or not. The waiting process had me nervous not knowing what news I would receive. I would check my personal email in the library or computer lab faithfully 3-4 times a day in hopes to see an email from Wells Fargo. After several weeks without knowing an answer, I finally received an email from the recruiter that read in a nutshell that they moved forward with another candidate for the position. I don't have to tell you how devastated I was, but what I will share with you is part of me felt as if I was a failure. I had completed four years of education and the one goal I needed to achieve, didn't happen.

At that point I became very frustrated not knowing what I was going to do. I didn't want to go back home to live. So, I decided to move in with my brother Kenny for a few months. The plan was simple, stay persistent every day calling and emailing job recruiters until I got hired somewhere. A month later, I received a call from Mrs. Jackson with an opportunity to do more than mentorship for her Summer Youth Leadership program at Benedict College. She wanted me to be one of the program coordinators which entailed putting together daily activities, college tours and job shadowing. I gladly accepted the position even though it was temporary. The summer job helped me earn some money while I continued to search, apply and interview for full-time jobs. When the door of opportunity is in front of you, don't hesitate to open and walk in.

In the midst of working my summer job, one of the managers from my second interview with Wells Fargo reached out to see if I was hired. He was shocked to find out I didn't get the Credit Manager position and insisted on helping me get hired as a Phone Banker. This position was in a call center which was not what I dreamed of doing after college but I needed a job. The manager from my second interview called a recruiter to pull my resume for the Phone Banker position. The recruiter was impressed and called me to do a phone interview. I knocked it out the park and was asked to do an in-person interview a few days later. This time around I was ready! I wasn't going to lose twice.

I arrived at the interview with my black suit, black shoes, white shirt and gold tie. My mindset was to make a great impression and I believe I did. Once I finished the interview, I was told a decision would be made in a few weeks. To my surprise, I received an emailed from Wells Fargo several days later. YES, I was excited but afraid to open the email. I didn't want to face another disappointment. It took a few minutes to mustard up enough courage to open and read it, but I'm glad I did. The letter informed me I was hired for the Phone Banker position. That process taught me failure is not valid until you quit. The manager who helped me get the job taught me a key principle; make your first impression with everyone unforgettable. The simple truth is there's power in your decision to stay persistent even when you don't know what the outcome will be.

Think about a time when you accomplished something that at first did not seem attainable. You had no idea how to reach that goal, just a burning desire to achieve it. For example, finishing high school, college, saving money for your first car, buying your first house, becoming an entrepreneur or finding a job. Believe it or not, your persistence is what brought you through countless rejections and setbacks. You had such a belief in what you were doing that no doubt, fear, challenge or obstacle could stop you from succeeding! Whatever goals you're pursuing now, don't forget the power that guided you before.

I believe having knowledge, talent and skill is not what gets you to a certain level of success. They are important. However, persistence is an essential trait to succeed. Look at the great Dr. Martin Luther King Jr.; he's a hero to many people because of his ability to persist beyond opposition. What if he would have quit after his first, second or third failed attempt to change the hearts and minds of the American people? Thomas Edison is another perfect example of allowing persistence to prove anything is possible to the person that doesn't give up. It's said that Mr. Edison failed 10,000 times before eventually finding a way to invent the electric light bulb we all use today. He said in one of his famous quotes:

"Our greatest weakness lies in giving up.

The most certain way to succeed is always to try just one more time."

If you keep swinging an axe to a tree in the same spot, eventually it is going to fall. Persistence rewards the individual who doesn't quit. The problem is people quit not knowing exactly how close they are to finishing what they started.

There's always a finish line waiting on you to cross. You may be exhausted or frustrated right now but I'm challenging you to PUSH through your pain. Fight through life's barriers and road blocks using the power of persistence every step of the way. The nucleus of every achievement is persistence. The success stories of some of the most prominent people of our history share a common denominator, persistence. They never gave up or stopped trying on their journey to change the world. The reason your favorite celebrity is so successful and famous because they were willing to knock on the door of their dreams, more times than someone else was willing to knock on theirs. You're where you are today because of your unrelenting attitude to keep going when others chose to quit.

Three Ways to Help You Stay Persistent

Find the purpose behind your goal

Once you set a goal, don't take action until you have a deep-rooted reason WHY that goal needs to be accomplished. The source of motivation to stay persistent and determined to finish your process is your BIG why. The reason most people quit on their journey to success is they don't have a strong enough reason to keep pressing forward. If you rely on the BIG why no obstacles can stop you from succeeding.

Never Stop Visualizing the Success You Want

I was able to finish this book because I continuously imagined myself giving my mom her first copy, doing my first book signing in my hometown, traveling doing book tours and staying up late signing autographed copies to ship to customers around the world. When you need that extra boost, find that inspiration and motivation through visualizing where you want your life to be 4, 8 or 12 years from now. Don't limit yourself. It costs you nothing to dream.

Stay Focused

Write your goal down and don't go a day without seeing it. When you know what you want and make it the center of your attention, you're more likely to stay persistent towards achieving it. Always remember where your focus goes, the mind and body will follow. Keep your mind on your ambitions and away from all negativity. Stay focused!

Average to Awesome Success Tip

Build a habit of staying persistent towards a goal you've set. Discipline yourself to give a (set time) each day to work on that goal. Don't deviate from the success plan you've developed because it gets too hard. Stay the course and keep grinding!

Questions to Consider

1. Persistence has helped many people achieve success. Now that I have read this chapter, how can persistence help me succeed?

____

____

____

____

2. If I stay persistent faithfully, what goal can I achieve in the next 30 days?

____

____

____

____

3. Tell a situation where you quit before you finished. How would being persistent have changed your outcome?

____

____

____

____

Chapter 8

Go Get It!

"Don't ever let someone tell you that you can't do something. Not even me. You got a dream, you gotta protect it. When people can't do something themselves, they're gonna tell you that you can't do it. You want something, go get it. Period."

–**Will Smith** (The Pursuit of Happyness, film)

When I first started working for Wells Fargo right after college, I was very hungry for success. I was a 23-year-old with a go-getter mindset. My position at the company was a phone banker, which really meant sales representative. I must admit, being confined to a desk selling financial products was not the vision I had for myself after college. My vision was to obtain a marketing job with a fortune 500 company where I could travel around the world making presentations and promoting the company's brand. I envisioned having a company car with all travel expenses paid. Sounds pretty cool right? Wells Fargo is a fortune 500 company, but there was no traveling involved. That didn't stop me from excelling as a sales representative. Learn to maximize every opportunity until you reach your destination.

After I was hired, I had to attend a mandatory sales training for several weeks to prepare me for my job duties. What excited me the most was the opportunity to become one of the top performing sales bankers in the call center and represent my sales team. I thought my first year making that happen would be incredible. My goal was set and I was ready to go! Once my training was over and it was time to perform, I was selling as if my life depended on it. Every chance I saw that my customer would benefit from one of our products, I offered it. On my team as well as throughout the call center, the stakes were high because it was extremely competitive, but I was up for the challenge.

Each week my manager would congratulate me on a job well done for meeting sales goals. I was elated that my name was being called. After several months of hard work and selling I was called into my manager's office to receive some great news. I was told my sales numbers met the criteria to receive the prestigious award of 1st Quarter Top Performer Sales Banker. All I could do was smile big like a baby being tickled. I realized in that moment one of the greatest feelings in the world was setting a goal and achieving it. The crazy part was I earned that award within a year of being with the company. My vision didn't manifest exactly how I wanted after college, but I continued pressing forward. It wasn't until I left Wells Fargo that my job with Thomas Media Group afforded me the opportunity to travel, promote advertising products and make presentations to business owners across the state of South Carolina. I'm here to tell you if you want something bad enough, don't just talk about it, go get it. Period!

The singer Beyoncé wrote a song called Formation that had all females yelling "iSlay." If you are a male reading this, my apologies brother! Stay with me please. In the chorus of that song and I'm paraphrasing, Beyoncé simply conveys with confidence that her grind will get her what she wants. A bold statement but her work ethic speaks for itself. What have you said you were going to do and have yet to take actions towards it? The dream is free but the grind, hustle and work comes from your own effort. Stop wishing for it and not think you will have to work for it.

I believe people become college graduates, world class professionals, savvy entrepreneurs, and rich and famous because they never allow failures to stop them from trying again or let one achievement stop them from accomplishing another. These are people who have an appetite for success and reaching new heights. Are you hungry enough to go out and grind persistently to change your life? If you have to go the extra mile for what you really want in life, DO IT! Your future self will thank you.

Stop sitting on your goals and dreams and watching superstars on TV live theirs. You should desire an abundant and prosperous life too. We all get 24 hours in a day to work on creating the life we envision for ourselves. We have to conquer each day God allows us to see. When your eyes open and feet touch the floor, it's game time! What you must realize is "sit down," is never going to tell anyone to get up. That means if you don't make a decision to change your life or take action towards the goals you've set, life will eventually pass you by and there will not be anyone to blame but yourself. One of Malcolm X's famous quotes says, "The future belongs to those who prepare for it today." Are you going to put off until tomorrow what you can prepare for now?

Urgency is a Major Key

Have you ever seen the sense of urgency from a dog that goes to fetch a bone or a ball? If you notice, once the dog owner's hand releases what the dog wants, there's no thinking involved, only reaction. It doesn't matter which way the object is thrown or the distance, the dog moves swiftly to go get it, right? If you are a dog owner, I can only imagine the workout you're giving your arm every time you throw the ball or the bone. Also, think about the cardio exercise you're giving your dog at the same time. Both of you are tired and drained once the playing is over. What's most important to know is when the opportunity presents itself, don't wait to take action; seize the moment right away. You never know when the job promotion, job opening or extra credit from your teacher or professor will come around again. Here's a key principle to remember: stop thinking and start reacting.

Failure is not Final

Going after success can lead to many failures. However, failure is not final. It's only a setback that's going to help you prepare for a comeback. I'm here to tell you whatever aspirations you have in life, it's going to take guts, heart and courage to not give up when you think you've given enough. You may stumble and even fall occasionally, but I encourage you get back up. Start your process towards changing your circumstances. Don't be afraid to fail. You're not the only one who's been down that road before and you will not be the last. In my Tupac voice, keep your head up!

Success is Earned Not Given

Nothing in life will be given to you. Everything you want has to be earned through hard work, perseverance and faith. I want you to chase success like a lion going after a gazelle. GO GET IT!

What did it take for athletes like Michael Jordan and Serena Williams to become successful at their game? Michael Jordan once stated, *"I've always believed that if you put in the work, the results will come."* Serena Williams once stated, *"Everyone's dream can come true if you just stick to it and work hard."* I believe it's not solely because of their talent that they're great athletes. I'm convinced it's their mental toughness and willingness to train, study and practice longer than anyone else. While other athletes are just trying to meet the expectations, they exceeded theirs. When you have a mixture of passion, determination and strong work ethic, you're bound to stick out like a sore thumb. The greats didn't become great by showing up. It was the preparation before the show that made them become a legacy worth remembering. I conclude that hard work beats talent any day of the week. It is a fact that you will encounter people that are smarter than you, more popular than you and have more titles than you, but none of that matters. Stay focus on your goals and don't let them outwork you!

Average to Awesome Success Tip

Stay consistent every day with the three G's, Get Up, Get Dress and GO GET IT!

Questions to Consider

1. What can I do differently to get the results I want in school, work or business?

____

____

____

____

2. What can I learn from my favorite celebrity to achieve the goals I've set?

____

____

____

____

3. What motivated me in this chapter the most? How can I use that motivation to accomplish my next goal?

____

____

____

____

Chapter 9

Someone Is Counting on YOU

"Your success is an insurance policy for someone else."

–Tim Bowers

I remember the words my nephew Cameron said to me on my college graduation day, "Uncle Tim, I wanna go to college too!" He was a young boy, but he saw something awesome I achieved that he wanted for himself. It was right in that moment I realized getting a college degree was no longer about me. It was about reshaping, breaking and creating a new path for generations coming behind me. How would it make you feel knowing your children, nieces or nephews watched you accomplished something awesome and they uttered the words afterwards, "I want to do what you did!" I don't know you, but I can imagine if you heard those words, it would melt your heart. You may be their only hope to believing their dream in life is not farfetched. Take a few seconds to think about who would be affected if you decided to give up on your dreams.

Write their name(s) below:

____

____

____

____

Whether you know it or not, there is someone counting on you to succeed. That someone may be your child, a family member or friend who is depending on you to achieve great success. The fact that you're striving to be awesome on this earth, serves as an inspiration for those who have a desire to be great as well. Your will to succeed alone gives those who are depending on you, permission to chase after the desires of their heart. What's most important for you to remember is never be naïve and think your journey to success is all about you, because it's not! You must realize that your future success is also someone else's motivation to become a success story one day.

When you consider the possibilities of what your achievements can do for others, you work harder to finish what you've started. The inevitable truth about pursuing success is that the process won't be easy. I believe when people know there's someone rooting for them to win, it compels them to continue pressing forward when the mind tells them to throw in the towel. If you've experienced this, then what you have is called a WHY. The reason for what you do is a powerful source to remind you that it's necessary to give more effort, time and energy towards the purpose.

Think about it from this perspective. In war, there is a team of soldiers who go out for battle. If one soldier gets injured in combat, that soldier needs help from his comrades to be carried for treatment in order to possibly make a return. When you've reached a point of despair in your life, don't abandon your process. Remember, you have someone (YOUR WHY) who has enough power to pick you up and motivate you to not give in or give up. Use your WHY as a resource for power to overcome the mindset of quitting. Below, list the people you love dearly that would be considered your WHY.

Write their name(s) here

____

____

____

____

Look at their name(s) at least three times a day.

It's Bigger Than YOU

Once you understand the dream you're working to make a reality is bigger than you, the work involved becomes purposeful. The moment I realized this book was not about me adding the title "author" beside my name, writing the chapters became less dreadful. My mind was considering the youth in my hometown community and around the world struggling through their process, needing inspiration and guidance to get through it. There are students who believe their dreams are impossible. There are millennials trying to climb the hills to reach another level of success and they are in need of someone to push them harder. Once I understood my intent to write the book, it impelled a reason for me to start the process and finish! When you become obsessed with the larger picture of your dream, the process becomes invaluable.

Believe in YOURSELF

On your path to greatness, see yourself where you want to be before you arrive. If you desire to be a college student, see yourself walking on the campus of that school. If you desire to become a millionaire, see yourself doing what millionaires do. If you desire to own your own business or become CEO of a company, see yourself in those positions. Remember this: you become what you believe. Don't stop believing in your ability to do what others think is impossible. Henry Ford said, "*Whether you think you can or you think you can't, you're right.*"

Don't expect people to believe in you, if YOU don't believe in yourself! Business mogul and rapper Jay Z said, *"Always believe you're great before anybody believes it."* If you don't believe in yourself, it's pointless to set goals. Don't pursue a dream until you believe in the dream. You have to believe in what you want before you can have what you want. This is the first step toward success.

Average to Awesome Success Tip

The key to overpower the thought of giving up is remembering why you started and who's counting on you to succeed

Questions to Consider

1. Why is it so important to finish what I've started after reading this chapter?

____

____

____

____

2. What have I learned about myself after reading this chapter?

____

____

____

____

3. What legacy do I want to leave on this earth for someone to remember?

____

____

____

____

Chapter 10

This is Your Time to S.O.A.R.

"Don't be a pigeon if you were born to be an eagle."

– Dr. Myles Munroe

CONGRATULATIONS! You've made it to the end of this journey. You've proven to yourself you can finish what you start. That's POWERFUL! This process to completion has prepared you to S.O.A.R. like an eagle NOW, not later! Take what you've learned from each chapter and **S**ecure **O**pportunities to **A**chieve **R**emarkable success!

It doesn't matter how you start, how you finish is most important. Sometimes you can't control the cards that were dealt to you, but you can control how you play your hand. As an adolescent teenager, I was always into something mischievous, whether at school or after school. My trouble record ranged from school disturbances, hitting a teacher, vandalizing property and poor academic performance. I was on the verge of failing 7th grade. I remember standing in front of Judge Armstrong with my mother not knowing what to expect. The judge had no sympathy for me, and at the age of 13, I was sent to the Department of Juvenile Justice. This is where I was told what to do and when to do it with no exceptions. I had to march in line to eat breakfast, lunch and dinner repeating the words, "LEFT, LEFT, LEFT, RIGHT, LEFT!" I couldn't eat breakfast in the morning unless my bed was folded at a 45-degree angle. I couldn't use the restroom without getting permission first. I couldn't sleep in or stay up late watching TV. My time and freedom was controlled by someone else and I didn't like it. I figured out at an early age being, "locked up" was not the future I wanted for myself.

I spent a portion of my 7th grade year away from school. Upon my return, I was told I couldn't come back. The school administration stated I had to finish my school year at Allendale County Alternative School. As my mother would say, "If you make your bed hard, you have to lay on it." Sometimes it takes going through something to help you see life on that side of the fence is not where you want to be. Right at that moment, while my back was against the wall and all the odds were against me, I became determined to bounce back. My decision was not to become another statistic and I went to work. Eventually, I climbed myself out of the ditch to return back to regular school on good behavior and upgraded my academic performance from a D to a C. I call that progress! This improvement helped me pass the 7th grade. From then to now, I've changed the history of my family tremendously: I became a first-generation college graduate, entrepreneur, speaker and now, an author! WOW! But, I'm neither different nor better than you. I just decided not to give up when my life looked messed up. The point is, regardless of what process you're going through right now, it's possible for you to beat the odds and come out on top!

Three Simple Ways to S.O.A.R.

1. **Be Committed to the Process.**
   Whatever you start, FINISH!
2. **Take Pride in What You Do.**
   Give 100% in everything you pursue! No Excuses!
3. **Be YOU!**
   Oscar Wilde said, *"Be yourself, everyone else is already taken."* Don't change who you are naturally just to please everyone. You were born with a unique gift that's supposed to stick out like a thorn.

Whether you are a student, young adult or millennial, having confidence in yourself is a major key. Without it, you will experience difficulty unleashing your full potential. Build your confidence by setting small goals to achieve. Once you accomplish one goal, set more and watch how your confidence increases over time. The simple truth is, you have greatness within you, but until you realize it, where you are is where you will always be. A person does not become awesome by reaching a certain level. A person becomes awesome when they have a dream and grind to make it a reality or set a goal and work to achieve it. Now is the time to make MORE moves and LESS announcements! Now is the time to REFOCUS on what's important, like your future! Now is the time to SEPERATE yourself from anything or anyone that's toxic in your life! Now is the time to become SERIOUS about taking your work ethic and mindset from average to **AWESOME!** If you really desire success, don't wait to start working towards it. **DO IT NOW!**

Your Life Has Purpose

Three major incidents happened in my life that helped me understand that my life had purpose. As I share these with you, reflect over your life in order to identify those situations that helped you realize your life has purpose too. The first one was with my childhood friends Marlon, Larry and Speedy. One day before we decided to go to recreation football practice, Marlon and I wanted to stop by the store to buy snacks. It was supposed to be Marlon and I on the bike while Speedy and Larry walked. However, Speedy thought it would be best for him to go instead of me. I said no at first, but Speedy was adamant about it so eventually I gave in and walked with Larry. While Larry and I walked, Speedy and Marlon took off on the bike headed to the store. Speedy rode the bike while Marlon sat behind him. As they turned off Pearl Street towards Water Street, Larry and I could still see them from afar. Before Speedy and Marlon could cross over Water Street, a truck came out of nowhere and hit them HARD! Larry and I watched it happen. We rushed to where they were and saw Marlon on the sidewalk and Speedy in the street with the back of his head bloody and busted open. We could tell Marlon was hurt but it wasn't as bad as Speedy. I stood there in shock as the thought ran across my mind, "is Speedy going to die?" The ambulance eventually arrived and took them to the hospital. However, Speedy had to get airlifted to another hospital who could handle the severe injury to his head. I watched the helicopter take my friend away not knowing what the outcome was going to be. I couldn't believe what transpired because I was initially supposed to be on the bike with Marlon, not Speedy.

The second incident was in college. My girlfriend at the time was from New York and she shared with me one afternoon that she needed a ride to the Charleston airport to handle some business back home. To be honest, I really didn't want to take her, but she was my girlfriend so I agreed to do it. Her flight was leaving really early one morning and I knew I would be tired on the road so I asked one of my fraternity brothers to ride with me. The time came for us to leave. I picked up my girlfriend from her dorm and my fraternity brother from the club and took Interstate 26 East towards Charleston. The drive to Charleston, South Carolina's airport from Columbia, South Carolina is approximately one hour and forty-five minutes. I thought the ride was going to be terrible but it wasn't. My girlfriend and I talked the entire way.

After I dropped her off to the airport, I asked my fraternity brother to drive back to Columbia. He agreed and shortly into the ride I dosed off to get some sleep. About 30 minutes outside of Columbia, I woke up suddenly to see my fraternity brother asleep and the car headed into the highway's safety wires. I shouted, "Bro, wake up!" He was scared and jerked the wheel to the right, which put us back on the highway in the lane where a van truck was coming directly on my side! The car was out of control! I looked over my right shoulder, saw the truck and turned my head because I knew it was over. It happened so fast, but at the right moment, my fraternity brother jerked the wheel back to the left and my car ended up crashing into the highway's safety barrier wire ropes. Once again, my life was spared!

The last incident hit home not just for me, but for people around the world. It involved the Emmanuel A.M.E. Church shooting. I had to work in Charleston that day with my helper Todd. We had to deliver the 2015-2016 South Carolina Black Pages to as many African-American churches in the "Holy City." What better place right? I knew I didn't want to be in Charleston all day, so the day before we left, I wrote down a list of churches we could make drops to of over 100 books or more.

Once we arrived, I notified the Charleston Black Pages Market Manager that we were headed to make our first drop. I talked over my list of churches with her and she indicated there were some businesses and churches I needed to add. She thought it would be better for us to make those drops first. However, my gut was telling me to stick with my plan and add her suggested places to the bottom of my list. Throughout the day, Todd and I made stops all across Charleston. We even made some stops at those suggested places mentioned by the Market Manager because they were not far from some of the delivery locations on my list. After delivering to over 12 churches, I remembered looking at the time, it was after 6pm and we still had a few hundred books left on the van. My plan to not be in Charleston all day turned out to be just that, all day! I received a call from the Market Manager to see if we were finished. I shared the estimated books I believed we had left and she quickly suggested several places we could go. We were already downtown and my gut instinct was to deliver the majority of the books to Mother Emmanuel and finish our day with those suggested stops the Market Manager gave us.

Todd and I followed our plan and went to Mother Emmanuel. We spoke with one of the members of the church to see where we could place the books. She told us where and left. I backed the truck closer to make our load-in easier to carry in. We dropped off several hundred books and left. After we completed all the churches on our list, Todd and I were elated to go home. I, as well as the world, found out later that night, Mother Emmanuel A.M.E. Church had a shooting where nine people were killed. My first thought was that Todd and I had just left the church less than three hours ago. God is AWESOME! The gunman entered the same door Todd and I used to bring in the South Carolina Black Pages. What if we would have made the decision to make Mother Emmanuel A.M.E. Church our last distribution stop? I'm not sure what would have happened, but Todd and I are thankful we didn't have to find out.

What those experiences did for me, especially the last, was give me more reasons to believe I'm here to do something phenomenal on this earth. When you really consider what you've been through and how far you've come, you start to make sense of how blessed you really are. I know the full picture of my purpose is still being developed, but I'm aware that part of my assignment is to inspire the youth, students and millennials on how to transition from where they are to where they want to be. In short, transform their lives from average to awesome. If you are not fully aware of your purpose now, find your passion and it will connect you to your purpose.

I believe we were not born to be average, rather born to leave a legacy worth remembering. What legacy will you leave behind? What will your peers, classmates and loved ones say about you when you're no longer here? You have people counting on you to succeed. Don't let them down. Use everything you've learned from this book to help you **S**ecure **O**pportunities to **A**chieve **R**emarkable success. From this day forward, become allergic to average and grind to achieve your level of awesome. You can do it as long as you believe you can!

WHEN I SAY **FROM,** YOU SAY **AVERAGE!**

FROM! ________________

FROM! ________________

WHEN I SAY **TO,** YOU SAY **AWESOME!**

TO! ____________________

TO! ____________________

Final Expectations

Tell a friend or a family member about what you've learned and encourage them to read "Average to Awesome."

Average to Awesome Success Tip

You must apply what you've learned or it becomes information that goes in one ear and out the next.

Questions to Consider

1. What's the most important lesson or principle I took away from this chapter? What area in my life can I apply it immediately?

____

____

____

____

2. What three commitments can I make to help me go from average to awesome?

____

____

____

____

3. What did I take away from this chapter that I can share to help my friends?

____

____

____

____

Motivating and inspiring quotes written by Tim Bowers

"Extraordinary doesn't happen until your expectations supersede the comfort zone of your mindset."

"Consider creating your own story. That way if anyone questions it, you're the source."

"You were not born to be average. You were born to leave a legacy worth remembering."

"Every day you wake up, you're the pen and life is your paper. Don't take the power you have lightly."

"If you want to change your life the first thing you must do is change the way you think."

"Do not neglect the gift that is in you. Find ways to utilize that gift because you never know whose watching."

"Don't change who you are naturally just to please everyone. You were born with a

unique gift that supposes to stick out like thorns."

"Don't run away from a challenge; allow complexity to unearth your creativity."

"You have to go after what you're trying to achieve like a baby learning how to walk and a child learning how to ride a bike. Don't stop until the goal set is accomplished."

"Don't forget that this is your life. Work hard to live it the way you envision it."

"Find your passion, which will connect you to your purpose, and the rest becomes history."

"You can't become who you were created to be until you let go who you're portraying to be."

"If you waste your life, don't get mad, you made the decision."

"Anything worth having is worth working hard to achieve."

NOTES

For more information on how you can bring Tim Bowers to your school, institution or next event, please go to www.timbowersspeaks.com

ABOUT TIM BOWERS

Timothy Andrew Bowers was born in Allendale, South Carolina, and educated in the Allendale County School District where he played football, ran track and participated on the high school debate team. Tim Bowers grew up at-risk where getting in trouble was the norm. He was expelled in middle school, sent to alternative school and served time in the Department of Juvenile Justice at the age of 13. His struggles and experiences; including an absent father, almost becoming homeless and watching his mother struggle financially gave him the motivation to achieve. Tim Bowers received his Bachelor of Science degree in Business Administration with a concentration in Marketing from Benedict College in 2010.

Tim Bowers changed the history of his family by becoming a first-generation college graduate. During his college matriculation, Tim was Senior Vice President of his class and was involved in various community service projects through his fraternity, Alpha Phi Alpha, Inc. In addition, he was awarded the David H. Swinton Presidential Service Award, which recognized his willingness to go above and beyond in service to the community. Currently, Tim Bowers is an Account Executive with Thomas Media Group, entrepreneur, author and motivational speaker with a focus on personal and student development. His aim is to help schools, colleges & universities position students for educational success and next level achievement. He lives by his own quotation: **"You were not born to be average. You were born to leave a legacy worth remembering."**

Made in USA - Kendallville, IN
85643_9781539899389
04.11.2023 1329